MEND MY
HEART

SHAUDAE SMITH

WESTBOW
PRESS®
A DIVISION OF THOMAS NELSON
& ZONDERVAN

WestBow Press books may be ordered through booksellers or by contacting:

WestBow Press
A Division of Thomas Nelson & Zondervan
1663 Liberty Drive
Bloomington, IN 47403
www.westbowpress.com
1 (866) 928-1240

ISBN: 978-1-5127-6793-3 (sc)
ISBN: 978-1-5127-6794-0 (e)

Library of Congress Control Number: 2016920242

Print information available on the last page.

WestBow Press rev. date: 4/10/2017

INTRODUCTION

I wrote this twelve-day devotional when I concluded that my heart needed to be mended after being damaged by so much junk I had allowed to consume it. I spent years allowing the wrong people to hurt me because I gave so much of myself to those who never measured up to my crazy expectations. I also felt abandoned by individuals whom I thought would be in my life forever, but I finally realized that they were never meant to be in my life past a certain season. They were there only to teach me lessons so that I could be molded into a stronger person. There were people I thought were my friends, but in hindsight, I know that most likely they couldn't have cared less about what happened to me. They sure didn't have a problem expressing their true opinions about me behind my back.

So many times I let different individuals disrespect me because I did not properly teach them how to treat me. Instead they learned they could overstep boundaries, because I never set limitations to guard my heart. I had friends I thought would grow old with me and be alongside me to share in various milestones and achievements throughout my life, yet I will never be able to share another moment with them, although I know they are with me and rejoicing in spirit. For years, I have held my feelings in, and it has taken a toll on my heart. For too long I have let all the wrong circumstances overtake me, and I have wasted too much time on all the wrong things that have left my heart bruised and wounded.

Unfortunately, I didn't know the damage I was causing by never dealing with my deep-rooted heart issues, but writing this devotional helped me really dig deep and find the cause of my brokenness, and tackle each problem one by one, so that the One who created my heart could repair it. The only way I could have my heart mended was by laying all my burdens on God and coming to terms with the fact that I could no longer try to take matters into my own hands. Honestly, I had never had control anyway. I no longer had the answers. I did not know where to start. I had to fall flat on my face and cry out to the One who knew me best, God. Only He knew how to mend my broken heart and make it whole again.

As I began to seek God through writing this devotional, He began to show me my weak areas that caused me to feel broken inside. He began to peel back the layers and reveal the issues of my heart. As I embarked on this journey, my eyes were truly opened to trouble areas I didn't even know I suffered from and couldn't get right on my own. I came to the point of admitting to myself that I had been harboring fear, bitterness, anger, discontentment, and much more. Indeed, I was broken. I was lost. I was far from feeling whole. I felt a void and distance from God because I had drifted so far from my Christian walk, which, honestly, hadn't been a true walk until this point of my life—the point where I needed God more than ever. My heart longed for something it was missing, but no one and nothing could fill that void.

As I began to grow in my Christian faith, God began to

reveal areas of my life that caused me to feel empty. I had to diligently seek the Word so that God could fix the problems I was experiencing. It was the only way to feel whole again. When I sought God's manual for repairing my heart, bits and pieces started to be mended. It was not an overnight process, and I constantly have to go back and fill up on the Word so that I can continue having my heart made whole. I can truly say that this has been and continues to be a journey that has made a tremendous difference in my life, and I want to share it with others who might be struggling with feeling like their heart is broken and who need God to make them feel whole once again or experience His love for the first time if they have never felt whole.

This devotional is for the brokenhearted. This is for those who feel as though no one loves them. This is for those who feel abandoned. This is for those who feel empty inside. Lastly, this is for those who have turned away from God, feel far from His presence, and will do anything to feel connected to Him once again. I pray that this twelve-day devotional touches your heart in the same manner it did mine when I was in a broken state: spiritually, mentally, and emotionally. As you go through each devotion, I ask that you really seek God and read each scripture, as well as complete each section challenge by journaling. That will allow you to take away the full message from each excerpt, because the words on these pages are not just for me; they are for you too. You also have a story, and as you complete each section challenge in its entirety, I am certain that your Christian walk and your relationship with Christ will be enhanced. It will point out areas that you struggle with and did not even know you needed to work on. I pray that this devotional will truly be a blessing to your life as it was for mine.

FREE FROM ANGER

DEVOTION

> Stop being angry! Turn from your rage! Do not lose your temper—it only leads to harm.
> —Psalm 37:8 NLT

> Slowness to anger makes for deep understanding; a quick-tempered person stockpiles stupidity.
> —Proverbs 14:29 MSG

> –Understanding this, my dear brothers and sisters: You all must be quick to listen, slow to speak, and slow to great anger. Human anger does not produce the righteousness God desires.
> —James 1:19–20 NLT

Anger is one of the many deceptive devices of the enemy. Many of us are filled with anger and do not even recognize the signs. Others are aware of their struggle with anger but do not know what the root issue is. However, if one struggles with anger, there is always a solution. Change might take time, and you might face many challenges reconstructing your emotions, but all things are possible if you have faith (Hebrews 11:1). The first step in making a change is believing in your mind that nothing is impossible, but there is a catch. Change begins in self, but no man is powerful enough to make such a drastic change without the help of the Lord. Yes, we must be open to change to move forward in life. However, once you have made up your mind that you want to be happy and put aside anger, it suddenly becomes a challenge for you to change. Once you encounter difficulty in trying to change for the better, your mind for some reason starts a war against your will, causing you to think it's impossible to do. Remember, with God all things are possible. So do not give up just yet! Keep pressing forward until you see change.

It is easy to be angry, and once you stir up that emotion, it is hard to take a step back, take a deep breath, walk away from the situation that is causing tension, and refrain from anger. Ephesians 4:31–32 says, "Get rid of all bitterness, rage, anger, harsh words, and slander, as well as all types of evil behavior. Instead, be kind to each other, tenderhearted, forgiving one another, just as God through Christ has forgiven you" (NLT).

It is understandable that it is hard to walk away from certain situations, especially from those our heart is passionate about, but walking in the flesh hinders our blessings. A person who walks away from a problem is a bigger person than the one who acts foolishly because of anger. Think about the crazy things people do out of anger. Some people say they black out when they are angry. Others say they see red. Someone else might use profane language or even become physically violent. None of these reactions are positive or godly, which means they entertain the enemy and do not, in any way, shape, or form, glorify Christ. Psalm 37:8 says, "Stop being angry! Turn away from your rage! Do not lose your temper—it only leads to harm" (NLT).

Anger will not always be provoked because of people; anger can also be manifested in individuals because they are truly unhappy or angry with themselves. When one is angry from regret, it is redirected and put off on others. It is easy to blame others for things that are wrong in our lives, but it is hard to accept responsibility for our own actions. After all, most things we are not happy about are there because we never tried to change our circumstances. We just chose to accept negativity and stayed in the same position because we felt like no good would ever come from the things that seem to constantly go wrong. As stated before, you must believe things will change. Once you believe and continue to have faith that things will work out for the better, results will actually begin to produce positive outcomes in your life. We do create some of the horrible circumstances that we face, but we can overcome and correct situations if we still have life. Remember, as long as you still have life, you still have a chance to get it right.

Of course, changing is easier said than done. Thinking positively is also more difficult than thinking negatively, because thinking positively requires work. Most people hate to do work; instead they choose the lazy route and stay in the same circumstances. This way of thinking blocks individuals from realizing that everything of value requires work and is worth fighting for. Fight to be better. Fight to be happy. Fight for change. Let go of angry thoughts that hinder you from moving forward. When you feel anger rise up and feel like you need to express how you feel, take a moment and think about James 1:19–20 and Proverbs 15:18.

Although you might make up your mind that you are

choosing to change and decide you will no longer walk in the spirit of anger, you will be tested to see if you continue to fight for change or give into the devices of the enemy. Choose to fight, and believe that your fight will be worth it in the long run. According to Proverbs 14:29, "People with understanding control their anger; a hot temper shows great foolishness" (NLT).

Once you feel a change and it seems like you are no longer walking in the spirit of anger, you might notice a difference in how you think. You will notice that you are starting to think positive, happier thoughts, but all of a sudden you might become angry because you began to smile. The funny thing is, once you notice you are choosing to be happy, you can sometimes become angry because you no longer feel the spirit of anger. If God is trying to help you move forward and deliver you from the spirit of anger, then why are you trying to hold on to the devices of the enemy? "One who is wise is cautious and turns away from evil, but a fool is reckless and careless. A man of quick temper acts foolishly, and a man of evil devices is hated" (Proverbs 14:16–17 ESV).

If you continue to satisfy and give in to the spirit of anger, your anger will soon trickle from anger and produce a greater negative result, called bitterness. Colossians 3:8 says, "But now ye also put off all these: anger, wrath, malice, blasphemy, filthy communication out of your mouth" (KJV). Maybe the things you are saying out of your mouth to others are the things you feel or think about yourself. Be careful of the tricks of the enemy, for it is he who wants us to live with angry thoughts so that we can eventually have hate in our hearts. Instead, follow after positive thinking and "put on the new man, which is renewed in knowledge after the image of him that created him" (Colossians 3:10 KJV).

JOURNAL CHALLENGE

Check your heart! Are you holding on to a situation or situations that have made you extremely angry? Think about a time when anger got the best of you. How did you react in that moment? Does that situation or do those situations continue to affect you today? After reading this devotional, how do you think you could have handled that situation or those situations differently?

LETTING GO OF BITTERNESS

DEVOTION

–Getting rid of all bitterness, rage, anger, harsh words, and slander, as well as all types of evil behavior. Instead, be kind to each other, tenderhearted, forgiving one another, just as God through Christ has forgiven you
—Ephesians 4:31–32 NLT

–Work at living in peace with everyone, and work at living a holy life, for those who are not holy will not see the Lord. Look after each other so that none of you fails to receive the grace of God. Watch out that no poisonous root of bitterness grows up to trouble you, corrupting many. Make sure no one is immoral or godless like Esau, who traded his birthright as the firstborn son for a single meal. You know that afterward, when he wanted his Father's blessing, he was rejected. It was too late for repentance, even though he begged with bitter tears.
—Hebrews 12:14–15 NLT

In the previous passage, I talked about anger. Although anger and bitterness are similar, bitterness tends to be a sneakier emotion. It's a deep-rooted and underlying feeling that we sometimes do not even realize exists within us. We thought we had stopped being angry, but something reminds us of a person or a situation we were once angry about, and all of a sudden we can't shake that emotion any longer and the same old bitter feelings rise again. It is then when we realize that we are still holding on to the past and finally have to admit to ourselves that we are not quite over things. Nine times out of ten, it is because we have not truly dealt with the situation and have let anger fester into bitterness somewhere along the line.

My struggle with bitterness stemmed from poor decisions I had made in the past. I would have days when it seemed like all I could do was think about all the wrong I had done and all the wrong people I had been involved with. There were certain job opportunities that I wish I had taken advantage of before I graduated from college. I started to have feelings of regret and ask "what-if" questions. Just the past in general had a negative effect on my present state of mind. I felt like sins I had committed had brought me to a place of drastic change in my life. It seemed as if once I graduated, everything changed at once in an extreme way. My choices in life affected not only me, but others around me. Feelings of shame, guilt, and hatred toward myself began to turn into feelings of bitterness toward others and myself without my realizing it. I understood that decisions in life always had consequences, but I had become so overwhelmed by the lasting effects of my decisions that I had become angry beyond measure.

There were days when it seemed like I was just starting

to go from feeling like I was on the path of success to feeling like I had failed myself completely. I had gotten a degree and had worked hard at everything I had done. I tried breaking out of my shell when it was necessary. I even surpassed a few personal goals I had set for myself, but I was still bitter— bitter because everything seemed to be falling apart and I was so far from where I thought I should be at that point in my life. I felt stuck, and my biggest fear in life had become my reality. My biggest fear in life used to be that I would be "a failure," yet that seemed to be the very thing I had succeeded in becoming. Here I was, with a job that I wanted to make a full-time career, but it did not provide steady pay. Bills, bills, and more bills piled up. I had school loans up to my neck. I was far from where I had imagined my life to be at that point of my journey.

I had a lot of bitterness from my overwhelming sense of failure and became even more annoyed when I looked at others around me who seemed to have it all together. I was not angry that they had things going for them, because I would not wish ill on anyone, but it created questions of why? Why couldn't things go well for me? Why couldn't I find my dream job with the pay that I desired? Although I loved working my job, it did not feel like it was enough. Just why? Why? *Why* syndrome had overtaken me. There were moments when bitterness consumed me so much that I would have rather been dead than deal with how I was feeling.

Eventually, the bitterness monster bit me so hard that it became the bane of my existence. I had even become angry with God, because I could not understand how He had let my life get into such a funk. I didn't understand why I was living, because I no longer felt like I had purpose. I would question why He was not changing my current circumstances when He knew they were killing me spiritually and emotionally. I was bitter because it didn't seem like He was answering my prayers or showing me what to do in this season of my life. It felt like He had abandoned me. I knew I had to go through a process and that in this life we will face tribulation, but I wanted my testing period to come to a halt. I felt like for once I was living up to my promises that I had vowed to Him, but it did not feel like He was showing His mercy on me. I had an attitude as if God had owed me something, but all He was trying to do was get my attention to help me understand that I was focusing only on the smaller picture. God was trying to show me that I had to let go of the past and handle my emotions before He could restore blessings into my life.

Bitterness is a deep-rooted heart issue that only God can fix. If we do not get to the root of the problem, then it still lies within our heart. I realized that I had befriended bitterness and needed to let go of it once and for all. I finally recognized that my heart needed mending.

JOURNAL CHALLENGE

Check your heart! Have you been harboring bitterness in your heart? Began to reflect on a situation or situations that have caused you to feel bitter. Have a moment of prayer to ask for forgiveness, and ask God to cleanse your heart of any and all bitter feelings.

SELF-PITY THAT PRODUCES A FALSE SENSE OF SELF-WORTH

DEVOTION

Don't become so well-adjusted to your culture that you fit into it without even thinking. Instead, fix your attention on God. You'll be changed from the inside out. Readily recognize what he wants from you, and quickly respond to it. Unlike the culture around you, always dragging you down to its level of immaturity, God brings the best out of you, develops well-formed maturity in you.

—Romans 12:2 MSG

Then Jesus said, "Come to me, all of you who are weary and carry heavy burdens, and I will give you rest. Take my yoke upon you. Let me teach you, because I am a humble and gentle at heart, and you'll find rest in your souls. For my yoke is easy to bear, and the burden I give you is light."

—Matthew 11:28–30 NLT

A cheerful heart is good medicine, but a
broken spirit saps a person's strength.
—Proverbs 17:22 NLT

Have you ever gotten to the point of feeling completely
sorry for yourself? It seems like everything that could go
wrong in your life is definitely going wrong. Every door that
you thought would open is shut and bolted. Opportunities
that you thought would present themselves have become
completely unavailable. Every person you thought you
could count on has let you down or is nowhere to be found.
You haven't yet reached your goals, and it is well past the
deadline you set for yourself. Now, here you are with all your
unaccomplished dreams that have left you feeling worthless.

How did I get here? you ask yourself. Yet you can't find
the answer to your own question. You can't even remember
the exact moment you lost sight. You don't know when you
stopped dreaming, but you feel like you don't even know how
to move forward. *Where do I go from here? Do I even deserve a
better life?* It is amazing how we question every circumstance
in our life but don't take the necessary steps to help move
ourselves forward. No, you might not be able to check every
dream off your vision board. No, you might not have caught
your big break yet. You might not feel worthy or deserving
of a better life, but there is still hope.

God already knows every maneuver you plan to make,
and He knows just how to make all of your desires come to
pass. Stop flooding your mind with past mistakes you have
made. Stop speaking negative statements that block your
blessings. Stop wallowing in regret about things that you
cannot go back in history and change. Just because situations
have not worked out the way you thought they would or the

way you envisioned them coming to passthat doesn't mean they will not happen. It doesn't mean God has forgotten about you. Lastly, it doesn't mean that circumstances can't change to work out in your favor in the future. God is not an ungracious God. He wants you to succeed in life. He has a plan for you. He knows when you are able to handle His unmerited blessings. He knows the second, minute, and hour that He will release them. He certainly can make your situations work for your good and transform what you see as tragedy and turn it into a glorious testimony in an instant. Don't limit God just because you cannot see the bigger picture and do not understand how He works. Hold on to faith. Continue to trust in Him. He has everything under control. He only wants your heart. Leave the rest up to Him!

Don't give up on God, because He will never abandon you. For every "no," keep the faith that something will work out in your favor. For every "no," keep pushing forward and do something that will help elevate you to the next level. For every "no," keep trusting that it is just a temporary setback and a setup for God to place something better in your future. For every "no," believe that God has already placed someone in your life to turn that "no" into a "yes." You were not placed on this earth just to be here. You were placed here with a purpose. I am a living witness that the "no's" are just setups for the greater picture. They are the setups for your destiny and purpose.

JOURNAL CHALLENGE

Check your heart! Are circumstances in your life causing you to have self-pity? Have you prayed about those areas of your life? Take a moment to speak to God about the areas in your life that give you feelings of worthlessness. God wants you to know that He has everything already worked out. Continue to speak positively throughout the day, and thank God for changing your circumstances in advance.

PRIDE COMES
BEFORE THE FALL

DEVOTION

Pride goes before destruction, and
haughtiness before a fall.
> —Proverbs 16:18 NLT

Pride ends in humiliation, while humility
brings honor.
> —Proverbs 29:23 NLT

For if a man think himself to be something,
when he is nothing, he deceiveth himself.
> —Galatians 6:3 KJV

You adulterers! Don't you realize that
friendship with the world makes you an
enemy of God? I say it again: If you want
to be a friend of the world, you make
yourself an enemy of God. Do you think the
scriptures have no meaning? They say God
is passionate that the spirit he has placed

> within us should be faithful to him. And
> he gives grace generously. As the scriptures
> say, "God opposes the proud but give grace
> to the humble." So humble yourselves before
> God. Resist the devil, and he will flee from
> you. Come close to God, and God will come
> close to you.
>
> —James 4:4–8 NLT

Pride was the number one problem that kept me from walking in the fullness of God. I always felt like I was right about everything I did, because I could not and did not see where I was wrong and developed the wrong way of thinking. Furthermore, I never wanted to wave my white flag and admit that I didn't have the answers. I didn't want to admit that I did not have things all figured out, because I thought it made me look weak. I sure didn't want to admit that I needed help. This way of thinking really didn't hinder anyone but myself, because in a sense, my pride kept me from asking God for help when I needed Him the most.

Ultimately, my never wanting to ask for help caused me to forget to constantly seek God on a daily basis. It was not until I hit rock bottom that I realized that I needed God's strength. It was the moment when I felt a void from God that I realized my pride had been a big factor in causing me to fall. It caused me to do my own thing, go my own way, and try to conquer life with my own strength, which was leading me down the road of destruction. I was left on a path of darkness with not even a flashlight to see. It was in the darkness that I came to the conclusion that my pride had to be set aside. I had to call on God to help me through the valley and lead me to the light once again. My way left me broken. My way left me feeling empty. My way left me lost, and it was because God found me that I was able to understand that my pride was my biggest downfall.

We have to surrender our pride to Christ. He knows our future even when we cannot see the bigger picture. Laying down your pride is ultimately making way for God to lead you in every area of your life, and that enables you to live with full access to God's favor and blessings. It is when we learn to humble ourselves that God can begin to show us His plans for our lives. It is when we humble ourselves that Christ can speak to us. It is when we humble ourselves that we can really see God's faithfulness toward us and we can conquer more with Him than without Him.

JOURNAL CHALLENGE

Check your heart! Has pride been getting in your way or stopping you from seeking God? If so, then it is time to die to yourself and lay down the spirit of pride once and for all. Make way for God to fully move in your life. The only way to do that is to give Him full control. Write in your journal about areas in your life that have caused you to be prideful, and have a moment of prayer to surrender your pride to God.

BITTEN BY THE JEALOUSY MONSTER

DEVOTION

A peaceful heart leads to a healthy body;
jealousy is like cancer in the bones.
—Proverbs 14:30 NLT

For wherever there is jealousy and selfish
ambition, there you will find disorder and
evil of every kind.
—James 3:16 NLT

Jealousy is a dangerous attribute. It can cause you to act out of character because you wish you were in the position that another person is in. We look at what others have, and how they appear to be happy, but sometimes we forget that people allow us to see them only when they're in a good state or present themselves only in the way they want others to view them. We never really stop to think about what a person had to go through or is currently going through to obtain materialistic or counterfeit happiness. Sometimes the people we envy are the very ones who are hurting deep down inside.

They may wish someone could see past their false pretenses and share encouraging words to help build them up. Instead of being jealous of others, start rejoicing with others in their blessings.

There is no need to feel jealous of other people, because what God has for you is for you. Your blessings are just as great as the next person's. There is always someone on the outside who might be looking at you and what God has placed in your life, and envies your lifestyle. I'm sure if you ask someone around you, they will confirm how they wish they had some of your qualities, personality traits, or material possessions. You are great just the way you were created. You are wonderful regardless of the type of car you drive, the style of shoes and clothes you wear, and the level of education you have; whether you realize it or not, you have a lot to offer the world.

Jealousy is just a stumbling block that prevents us from sharing our great qualities and perspectives with others because we feel inadequate or as if we do not measure up to other people's expectations or statuses. Do not let jealousy hinder you in any area of your life. Jealousy is a choice. Choose to be content in the position you were given at this point in your life. Use what you have, such as talents, knowledge, resources, and so forth, and share your uniqueness with the world. You never know who will be inspired or changed by your being the best version of yourself.

Stop comparing yourself with others, because there can be only one you, and this world does not need carbon copies of the same prototype. When you learn to embrace yourself the way you were created and learn to be content with what God has already given you, then He can begin to open up other opportunities in your life. Pushing aside feelings of jealousy and feeling genuinely happy at others' success is what makes God happiest, and that's when He can start releasing blessings to you. God says to "rejoice with them that do rejoice" (Romans 12:15 KJV). He takes delight when we show love and compassion toward others, not hateful, bitter, and jealous feelings. When we rejoice with others, we choose to have characteristics like Christ, which is what God ultimately wants from us.

JOURNAL CHALLENGE

Check your heart! Have you ever felt jealousy toward someone? Why did you have that feeling of jealousy? God never wants us to be envious of others. If this is an area in your life where you have been struggling, I encourage you to write your feelings of jealousy in a journal and pray each day until they subside.

Prayer starter: God, please forgive me for harboring any feelings of jealousy toward others. Give me the strength to genuinely rejoice with others in their time of well doing.

DISCONTENTMENT CAUSED BY CONSTANT DISAPPOINTMENT

DEVOTION

But seek ye first the kingdom of God, and His righteousness; and all these things shall be added unto you.

—Matthew 6:33 KJV

How I praise the Lord that you are concerned about me again. I know you have always been concerned for me, but you didn't have the chance to help me. Not that I was ever in need, for I have learned how to be content with whatever I have. I know how to live on almost nothing or with everything. I have learned the secret of living in every situation, whether it is with a full stomach or empty, with plenty or little. For I can do everything through Christ, who gives me strength.

—Philippians 4:10–13 NLT

> And we know that all things work together
> for good to them that love God, to them
> who are the called according to his purpose.
> —Romans 8:28 KJV

> Be thankful in all circumstances, for this is
> God's will for you who belong to Christ Jesus.
> —1 Thessalonians 5:18 NLT

After a major transition in my life, I found myself in a state of discontent. Here I was, a few years after graduating college, working full time in retail and as a freelance video editor. Yes, I had always wanted a creative job doing something I absolutely loved, and for the first time ever, I had that. Unfortunately, it didn't necessarily come with the pay and benefits that I really wanted. It was not enough to pay off all my school loans and assist in paying my ongoing monthly bills. It didn't come along with a medical and dental benefits package, nor did it offer me a comfortable lifestyle on my own so that I could completely be the young, independent woman I had envisioned myself to be at this point in my life. I felt blessed to have the opportunity to work in a field that I could see turning into a career, but I was not content with the lack of security.

I wanted it all, and I did not want to have to continue to wait for things to happen. Up to then, I had had a rough time, because my life had seemed to drastically change. I was completely in the season of loneliness because God was shaping me into the woman He has called me to be. I had always had a limited number of friends, but I was in the season where I felt completely lonely, even when I was surrounded by people. It just seemed to be God, my family, and myself. At least that is what it felt like I had, and all that it felt like I could depend on, and even then, God had me in a place where I sometimes felt lonely even when I was surrounded by my family. You might ask, "Why would God make you feel lonely and isolate you from people?" It wasn't that God was making me feel lonely, but He was isolating me to mold and shape me so I could walk into the purpose He had designed for me.

He wanted me to understand that no one could make me feel whole, no one could fulfill the desires of my heart, and no one could provide for me except Him—not even my family. So in this season, I had no choice but to put all my trust and faith in Him, which was truly hard for me to do, because I had major trust issues. I had always considered myself as having faith, but it was in this season that I realized I lacked faith completely. I was miserable because I felt like I had no job, although in reality I had two jobs; they just weren't supporting me in the way I desired. I hated feeling lonely, and I longed to have true Christian friends who were trying to live for God in the way I was. God quickly made it clear to me that I was trying to put my faith in things and people who would always let me down.

This was a hard pill for me to swallow, but it was true. My happiness had been contingent on material things and people up until this point, but as soon as things didn't go my way or people let me down yet again, I would begin to sulk, as if the world had ended.

I was also finding myself in a state of discontent because everyone around me seemed to have it made. They seemed to be able to make moves and make things happen, whereas I felt like I was doing everything humanly possible, but nothing seemed like it was ever working out the way I desired. I felt like I had gotten to the point where I was putting all my trust in God and had nothing left to give. I would question God over and over again, and still nothing seemed to change. It just felt like the constant repetition of disappointment after disappointment after disappointment, and I just wanted it to end.

One day it finally hit me. I was sitting here day after day in a depressed state because I couldn't have my way. The reality was that I had a home to live in. I had food to eat. God provided me with clothes and a vehicle for transportation. He was blessing me with a means to make money to pay for essential bills and still have a few dollars to spare. He was blessing me with a family who had never left my side, regardless of the stupid mistakes I had made countless times. The more I really looked at my life and thought about every simple to large blessing and the numerous opportunities God had allowed me to obtain, the more I began to realize just how ridiculous my sulking was. I had been ungrateful after all that He had done for me even though I did not deserve any of it to begin with. God truly had mercy on me, and I had to learn the importance of being content in every situation, regardless of how hard it may be, because God had given me the opportunity to go through something so He could show His goodness to me once again.

JOURNAL CHALLENGE

Check your heart! Have you ever been discontent in any way? Has your discontent been triggered by multiple disappointments in your life? Have you prayed about the areas in your life with which you are not content? Do you think God can change your current circumstances? Take the time to journal areas in your life in which you have been discontent, and have taken God's blessings for granted.

TRUST BEYOND YOUR UNDERSTANDING: DARE TO TRUST

DEVOTION

Oh the joys of those who trust the Lord, who have no confidence in the proud or in those who worship idols.

—Psalm 40:4 NLT

Psalm It is better to trust in the Lord than to put confidence in man.

—Psalm 118:8 KJV

–Trust in the Lord with all your heart; do not depend on your own understanding. Seek his will in all you do, and he will show you which path to take.

—Proverbs 3:5–6 NLT

Greed causes fighting; trusting the Lord leads to prosperity.

—Proverbs 28:25 NLT

This is what the Lord says: "Cursed are those who put their trust in mere humans, who rely on human strength and turn their hearts away from the Lord."

—Jeremiah 17:5 NLT

How many times have you wanted something badly but weren't quite sure if it was attainable? You would hope for the best outcome but prepare for the worst just in case things did not pan out in your favor. Instead of trusting in God and believing that He knows best, it was just easier to prepare myself for being let down than to expect a blessing. Even when it is hard to understand certain situations, you have to hold on to God's promises and trust and believe that all things are working in your favor. You have to continue to push past doubt and trust His plans. He knows His plans for your life, but He wants to see if you are going to trust Him with all your heart and believe that He will not leave you or forsake you.

It is easy to treat God as if He were just like people who have let us down time and time again. Before we realize it, we end up acting as if God is like man. Sometimes we put more of our trust in people than we ever put in God. The problem with that is we do not allow God to prove His faithfulness to us. He will allow the impossible to be possible. Trust that He will always make a way when there seems like there is no way. Have faith that if it is His will, it will come to pass, whether we understand it or not. Then, and only then, will He be able to move in ways that exceed our expectations.

God is always waiting for you to "trust in him with all of your heart, and … not lean on your own understanding" (Proverbs 3:5 KJV). He is waiting for you to hang on to His every word, because if He said it, then He will do it. When are you going to put your trust in Him so that He can show you His faithfulness? How long are you going to let doubt continue to block your blessings?

JOURNAL CHALLENGE

Check your heart! Are you struggling with trusting God to bring you out of a situation or situations or with believing He will change some circumstances in your life? Write a list of three things or areas in your life that you are trusting God to change. Pray for these three areas for the remainder of this devotional. If you are up for it, make it a super challenge, and pray for each item on your list for a month. Each day, or week, write in your journal about the progress of each item on your list that God is changing in your favor. . Growing in certain areas, opportunities that become available, doors that start to open, and transitions are clear signs of God answering your prayers. Dare to trust God, and see where faith takes you throughout this 6-day, or one-month challenge.

LET THE PAST BE THE PAST: SOUL TIES

DEVOTION

–Don't you realize your bodies are actually parts of Christ? Should a man take his body, which is part of Christ, and join it to a prostitute? Never! And don't you realize that if a man joins himself to a prostitute, he becomes one body with her? For the scriptures say, "The two are united into one." But the person who is joined to the Lord is one spirit with him. Run from sexual sin! No other sin so clearly affects the body as this one does. For sexual immorality is a sin against your own body. Don't you realize that your body is the temple of the Holy Spirit, who lives in you and was given to you by God? You do not belong to yourself, for God bought you with a high price. So you must honor God with your body.

—1 Corinthians 6:15–20 NLT

–Don't team up with those who are unbelievers. How can righteousness be a partner with wickedness? How can light live with darkness? What harmony can there be between Christ and the devil? How can a believer be a partner with an unbeliever?

—2 Corinthians 6:14–15 NLT

You adulterers! Don't you realize that friendship with the world makes you an enemy of God? I say it again: If you want to be a friend of the world, you make yourself an enemy of God.

—James 4:4 NLT

And that means killing off everything connected with that way of death: sexual promiscuity, impurity, lust, doing whatever you feel like whenever you feel like it, and grabbing whatever attracts your fancy. That's a life shaped by things and feelings instead of by God.

—Colossians 3:5 MSG

I'm sure the majority of us have emotional, mental, and physical soul ties from past relationships. How do we break these ties? How do we move forward? This was something that was difficult for me. I didn't even understand the spiritual damage that I had caused myself from being involved with the wrong people. They were not wrong necessarily because they were bad individuals, but they were wrong in the sense that we were not equally yoked. People with whom I shared my time, my energy, and the physical aspects of my life were not trying to draw me nearer to Christ. Although I should have also used that time to help bring others to Christ, I was really abusing a sacred place in me: my heart. My heart was contaminated because I was storing fleshly love and desires there instead of giving it to God.

God emphasizes that "wherever your treasure is, there the desires of your heart will also be" (Luke 12:34 NLT). So if your heart is connected to individuals who are not trying to reach the same destination you are, you will struggle to sacrifice areas of your life that help build you up spiritually. When your heart is connected to unbelievers or maybe even believers who are not trying to live a godly lifestyle, then it becomes a spiritual war when you want to try to do the right thing, because you have attached yourself to strongholds. Eventually, our past creates this enslavement to areas in our lives from which it becomes hard to separate ourselves without the help of God: lust, abandonment, lack of love, bitterness, unforgiveness, rape/molestation, insecurity, and so much more.

We hide these issues in our hearts instead of giving them over to the creator of our hearts. The one who can restore and rebuild. The one who can nurture and transform. The one who can fill the void and immerse you in an abundance of love. The one who loves all of your flaws and can heal every wound from people who took advantage of you. It doesn't matter what your past looks like. It doesn't matter whom you have connected yourself to. God's ways are not your ways. He wants to restore your heart, but you have to take the necessary steps and give Him the issues of your heart; then He will create in you a clean heart.

Your past does not define you. Stop holding on to your

past. What has happened in your past does not determine your future. Even if you feel like you are a lost cause, God knows how to use your story for His glory. You have a purpose. God has a plan. Give Him your heart, and He will give you a future beyond what you can ever think or imagine.

JOURNAL CHALLENGE

Check your heart! Have you connected yourself to people or things that have abused you spiritually, mentally, physically, or emotionally? What those individuals meant for your bad, God can turn into a glorious love story. He can mend those areas in your heart that are broken. He can loose the strongholds that try to attach themselves to you. Give God the issues of your heart.

Prayer Starter: God, forgive me for sharing the sacred parts of me that belong to You with others who were not deserving of my time and separated me from You. Cleanse me from any strongholds that have attached themselves to me so that I can be connected to You in a way like never before. Help me to move forward, and restore me. Thank You for loving me even when I have given myself to things and people who were trying to pull me away from You.

FORGIVENESS TOWARD OTHERS AND FROM GUILT

DEVOTION

–In prayer there is a connection between what God does and what you do. You can't get forgiveness from God, for instance, without also forgiving others. If you refuse to do your part, you cut yourself off from God's part.

—Matthew 6:14–15 MSG

–Then Peter came to him and asked, "Lord, how often should I forgive someone who sins against me? Seven times?" "No, not seven times," Jesus replied, "but seventy times seven."

—Matthew 18:21–22 NLT

Be gentle with one another, sensitive. Forgive one another as quickly and thoroughly as God in Christ forgave you.

—Ephesians 4:32 MSG

Forgiveness was always a touchy word for me. Why did I have to be the one to forgive others when they were the ones who had wronged me? I didn't want to be the bigger person. I wanted to hold on to the anger that I felt toward everyone who had ever treated me unkindly. I wanted to wrong them the same way they had wronged me, but worse. I wanted to hurt them the way they had left me feeling hurt. I wanted them to see how I felt, but for some reason I knew deep down in my heart that getting revenge would never make me feel better. Of course it would put a smile on my face in that moment, but I would only feel bad about it later on. Why is it that forgiveness is easier said than done? Even when I really thought I had let go of hard feelings toward others, there were times when I realized I still carried hurt and bitter feelings in my heart.

I had always viewed forgiveness as an act of weakness. I never really stopped to think about how forgiveness is also one of the first steps in our healing process—especially when we are trying to get over bitter feelings of being hurt and let down. I think we neglect to realize the power in forgiveness. My struggle with forgiveness toward others was only a portion of my issues. I was so angry about so much I was holding inside my heart that I didn't even realize that the biggest part of my healing process so that I could move forward was not just about forgiving others, but ultimately about forgiving myself.

I never understood that sometimes the reason we can't forgive others is that we do not know how to first forgive ourselves for past mistakes we have made. We don't forgive ourselves for inviting the wrong people into our lives. We don't forgive ourselves for letting people take advantage of us. If we don't know how to forgive ourselves, how will we ever know how to forgive others (Luke 6:31 NLT)?

Guilt can consume you and cause you to feel as though you are unworthy of love, blessings, or forgiveness. I personally struggled with feeling like I was undeserving of anything, including being alive, because of past sins I had committed. Guilt is a heavy burden for anyone to carry, and it is the number one thing that holds us back from forgiving ourselves. Let your past be your past. God permitted you to go through your mistakes so that you could learn how to deal with certain situations differently in the future. He already knew what decisions you were going to make and what detours you would take along your journey. He does not hold your past against you. Once you choose Him and live your life the way He has created you to, He will "have compassion upon us; he will subdue our iniquities; and thou wilt cast all their sins into the depths of the sea" (Micah 7:19 KJV). If Christ can forgive you of your past, then why can't you forgive yourself? None of us are deserving of His love or forgiveness, but because of His grace and mercy, they come along with His package, because He cares so much for you.

Forgiveness is not a suggestion but a requirement. When we choose not to forgive, we are only hurting ourselves. God clearly lets us know that if we cannot forgive others of their faults, it's hard to conceive of how He can forgive our trespasses (Ephesians 4:32 KJV). We have hurt God in more ways than we can count on two hands, and yet He sees fit to forget all the wrong we have done so that we can have everlasting life; how could we not extend that same forgiveness to others? Don't hinder your blessings because you choose to not forgive others. Instead, forgive, and free yourself of the burden, agony, and torment that comes along with not forgiving, including forgiving yourself. If God could forgive me for my countless filthy sins, who am I not to forgive others?

JOURNAL CHALLENGE

Check your heart! Do you find it hard to forgive others after they have hurt you? Are you still holding a grudge toward someone?

Prayer Starter: Father, forgive me for not forgiving others for hurting me. Your Word says, "If I do not forgive others their trespasses, neither will my heavenly father forgive me." So I ask You this day to strengthen me to forgive others and heal the areas in my life where I have been hurt. Mend my heart. Help me let go of the past entirely. I choose to forgive, so I ask You to help me move forward and never look back.

ENDURE WITH PATIENCE

DEVOTION

–For you know that when your faith is tested, your endurance has a chance to grow. So let it grow, for when your endurance is fully developed, you will be perfect and complete, needing nothing.

—James 1:3–4 NLT

Rejoice in our confident hope. Be patient in trouble, and keep on praying.

—Romans 12:12 NLT

Better is the end of a thing than the beginning thereof: and the patient in spirit is better than the proud in spirit.

—Ecclesiastes 7:8 KJV

Patience is built upon faith. Once people choose to believe that the trials and tribulations they are facing in their life are going to get better if they hold on to faith, then they also have to learn the value of patience. According to James 1:3–4, "the trying of your faith worketh patience. But let patience have her perfect work, that ye may be perfect and entire, wanting nothing" (KJV). Yes, you might pray over and over again about the same thing so often that you believe it will happen, but somewhere along the lines we forget that situations never work out in our timing. Romans 12:12 says, "Rejoicing in hope; patient in tribulation; continuing instant in prayer" (KJV). No matter what, we have to continue to pray for a greater finish until we overcome our struggles.

It is hard to keep patient when everything in your life seems to be working against you, but you must believe God will fix your situation. "But they that wait upon the Lord shall renew their strength; they shall mount up with wings as eagles; they shall walk, and not faint" (Isaiah 40:31 KJV). A lot of times we think we have the answers and know what is best for ourselves. We think to ourselves, *I have been going through this situation so long and endured so much that it is time for my blessings to be released,* but that is just like telling God you are in control of your life. We need to learn to let God be the head of our lives and trust and follow His direction. Trust me, when you do this, a weight will be lifted off your shoulders. All of your burdens will feel lighter and you will be able to see God move in ways that you never could have imagined. Philippians 4:19 says, "But my God shall supply all your need according to his riches in glory by Christ Jesus" (KJV). God will never fail us if we put our trust and faith in Him. As a matter of fact, He wants to bless us. He is just waiting for us to build a relationship with Him and be patient and believe that He will work all things in our favor.

Patience is never an easy trait, but "better is the end of a thing than the beginning thereof: and the patient in spirit is better than the proud in spirit" (Ecclesiastes 7:8 KJV). God has a time that He chooses to release our blessings. He knows all, and He will never give us more than we can bear. Think about faith like a job. When we have a job, we do not just get rewarded. We have to get prepared for work, drive to our work location, and clock in to show that we really did labor and earn a paycheck, and eventually we receive the check for our hard work. That is how faith is designed—just like a job. First, you have to believe that your situation will change (preparation stage). Next, you have to continue to speak and decree that your situation will change for the better (the vehicle to your breakthrough). In addition, you have to step out in faith and put in the work by continuing to pray, brainstorming positive ways to change your circumstances, and networking with people and using resources already provided to you until you reach your breakthrough (laboring stage). Finally, once God sees that you have endured the tests and trials He has placed before you, you will reap blessings (your reward) because you were patient and stuck through the hard times. Galatians 6:9 says, "And let us not be weary in well doing: for in due season we shall reap, if we faint not" (KJV).

Keep thinking positive thoughts even when nothing seems to be working in your favor. "Be careful for nothing; but in every thing by prayer and supplication with thanksgiving let your requests be made known unto God" (Philippians 4:6 KJV). Do not stop praying about your circumstances, but rejoice for your breakthrough. The sky might look gloomy right now, but soon the sun will shine. Remember God knows our finish, and He knows what is best for us even when we do not understand. "For I know the thoughts that I think toward you, saith the Lord, thoughts of peace, and not evil, to give you an expected end" (Jeremiah 29:11 KJV).,

JOURNAL CHALLENGE

Check your heart! Do you struggle with having patience in troubling times? Think about a time when you wanted something to work out instantly but God worked it out in His timing. When it came to pass, did it exceed your expectations? If our blessings are given to us prematurely, they can die, but when our blessings are given to us when God knows we can handle them, they mature and flourish.

A LOVE THAT IS TRULY UNCONDITIONAL

DEVOTION

If anyone boasts, "I love God," and goes right on hating his brother or sister, thinking nothing of it, he is a liar. If he won't love the person he can see, how can he love the God he can't see? The command we have from Christ is blunt: Loving God includes loving people. You've got to love both.

—1 John 4:20 MSG

–If I could speak all the languages of earth and of angels, but didn't love others, I would only be a noisy gong or a clanging cymbal. If I had the gift of prophecy, and if I understood all of God's secret plans and possessed all knowledge, and if I had such faith that I could move mountains, but didn't love others, I would be nothing. If I gave everything I have to the poor and even sacrificed my body, I could boast about it; but if I didn't love others, I would have gained nothing. Love is patient and kind. Love is not jealous or boastful or proud or rude. It does not demand its own way. It is not irritable, and it keeps no record of being wronged. It does not rejoice about injustices but rejoices whenever the truth wins out. Love never gives up, never loses faith, is always hopeful, and endures through every circumstance.

—1 Corinthians 13:1–7 NLT

We all search for love, but for some reason the majority of us look for love in all the wrong places. We look for love to replace the lack of love from our fathers and/or mothers. We look for love in people who are equally broken and searching for the same love and have the same void we are trying to fill. Somewhere along the search we just become even more lost. We become more broken. The void becomes greater, and before we know it, we no longer have love to share with anyone else.

I grew up in a two-parent household. My father is the model of a good man. He has worked all his life to take care of my mother, my little sister, my little brother, and myself. At times it was hard for him to provide for our family, but he never walked out, he never gave up, and he always tried his best to make sure my family and I felt loved. He is a godly man, and he has always treated me, as well as my family, with respect. He always let me know that I was valued and should not settle for anything less than the best.

That brings me to my next role model, my mother. A strong woman who knows how to hold her own if she needs

43

to, she always taught me how to believe in myself and have self-confidence. She is a stay-at-home mom and never missed a beat. Even when I made horrible decisions, both my parents stood by my side and helped lift me up once again. They helped me understand that mistakes are just lessons that make us stronger. We learn from them, keep it moving, and do better the next time around. At times I thought they would flat-out disown me because I knew they did not agree with the way I was living my life, but they never turned their noses up at me. Instead, they made more of an effort to show me love. There were countless times when both my parents sacrificed their wants and needs to make holidays and birthdays feel special for my siblings and me, when they could have easily just decided to be selfish and concentrate on themselves.

My parents are the ones who showed me what love was supposed to look like. Although I knew they loved me, I really struggled with feeling like I deserved it. I had made many mistakes throughout my life, and I knew my Christian faith had suffered severely because of my choices. My parents have always instilled good moral values in me, but somehow I had strayed far from the way they had raised me. I felt distant from God and as though He was incapable of loving someone like me—a person who deliberately chose sin over living for God, although I knew how much He hated the sin I was involved in. I was selfishly thinking only about myself and never about how I could or would hurt others around me.

I never understood why God extended grace to me or how He could forgive me for my shortcomings. I spent many days searching for God's love but never realized that His love had never changed. He loved me in the midst of my mess—so much that He saved me. When I was lost, He found me and brought me out of darkness. He allowed me to experience what life was like with Him, so that I could appreciate all that He had done for me and continues to do for me. More importantly, He allowed me to understand what life without Him feels like so that I would hold on to Him even more tightly now that He had given me countless chances to get it right.

Although I felt distant from God, He hadn't gone anywhere; it was I who had walked away from Him. Still, His love was shown to me through my parents' loving embrace—the same way my parents forgave me over and over again, the same way they never made me feel guilty for my wrongdoing. That was the same way God had extended His love to me, and why wouldn't He? After all, He is my heavenly father. He loves me because I am His, and when I walked away, He was right there waiting for me to return, His arms wide open, ready to embrace his daughter once again. This time I was never going to let go of His love ever again.

It is because of God and the wonderful family with which He has blessed me that I know what real love looks like. Although having my family's love is a great feeling, one thing I came to understand more than ever was that without the love of God, you can still feel empty, but when you have the love of Christ, you are made whole.

JOURNAL CHALLENGE

Check your heart! God's love is something that is hard to grasp. Time and time again He points out the importance of displaying love and requires us to love others the same way He loves us. Love is the number one characteristic of Christ, and if we are made in His likeness, love should be the main characteristic we show to others.

Prayer Starter: God, help me to love others the way that You love the world. I want to have a heart like Yours, and since Your Word commands me to love others the way I love myself, I want to be pleasing in Your sight and obey You in every way. Help me with this area of my life so that others can see the love of Christ dwelling inside of me.

YOU CAN MOVE FORWARD

DEVOTION

But forget all that—it is nothing compared to what I am going to do.

—Isaiah 43:18 NLT

"My thoughts are nothing like your thoughts," says the Lord. "And my ways are far beyond anything you could imagine."

—Isaiah 55:8–9 NLT

Therefore if any man be in Christ, he is a new creature: old things are passed away; behold, all things are become new.

—2 Corinthians 5:17 KJV

Don't copy the behavior and customs of this world, but let God transform you into a new person by changing the way you think. Then you will learn to know God's will for you, which is good and pleasing and perfect.

—Romans 12:2 NLT

There comes a time in every Christian's life when they realize they are lost. That point for me was my senior year in college. I was involved with various things that were utterly displeasing to God. I knew God was trying to get my attention and slowly dropping warning signs that I needed to remove myself from certain situations that I was holding on to that would send me straight to hell if I did not change my ways. I remember going to church on a Sunday in April 2014, and feeling God tugging on my heart to rededicate my life to Him. I stood there and kept reasoning with Him by thinking that I would give my life over to Him as soon as I "got myself together," but I didn't want to make that commitment and then turn around and indulge in the same selfish sins. I decided I would just wait, and I left the church service that day and did not respond to or heed God's warning.

As that day went by, a series of problems arose for me that I never thought I would have to face. Those were also the moments that put my Christianity into perspective. For a long time I was a "convenient Christian." You know the type: the Christian who professes to be a Christian, but nothing in their life lines up with God's Word. The Christian who tries to invite others to come to church—but why would anyone want to find out about Christ when the ones who are proclaiming to be Christians are in the club and taking shots to the head with them on the weekends? The type of Christian who falls to his or her knees and cries out to God only when he or she is in trouble. Yes, I was truly a "convenient Christian" and didn't understand what it meant to be a true Christian. It was definitely during this season of test and trials that I began to understand what a true Christian looked like.

I had to surrender all of my heart to Christ and let Him

lead the way. No longer could I try to be in control of my life, because truthfully, no matter how hard I tried to be in control, I would never succeed anyway. In the process, my faith and trust were tested over and over again. God had begun to show me that I was lost even when I didn't realize it and thought I had it all together. I was far away from God's presence and even felt the void, and I still didn't know I was lost. It was in that moment that God allowed what felt like everything to be snatched away from me. He allowed me to be broken so that He could rebuild, reshape, and restore me into the woman of God that He had called me to be, to help me get the revelation of what it meant to live life His way.

God had to remind me that just because I was lost, it didn't mean He had forgotten about me. Yes, it was going to be a process to get back into His presence again. It was going to take time, because nothing works in our timing, but His timing is what produces successful results. No, the process will not always be easy and fun, but it is necessary to really learn from our past mistakes. Our ways are not God's ways. Our understanding cannot compare to God's understanding. He knows all and sees all. Our idea of having it all does not even compare with the blessing that God has in store for us. We get stuck thinking we want things, but many times, if God gave us exactly what we prayed for, we would end up blocking the blessing He had in store for us that was far better than what we would ever ask for. God gives us seasons of hardship not because He hates us or forgot about us, but because He is reshaping us to get us ready for the next level in life. Are you passing the test, or are you getting impatient and failing the same level over and over again? Just hold on regardless of the situations you might be facing. God has not forgotten about you. You might feel lost, but you're not hopeless.

Sometimes your past or present circumstances aren't easy, but they are necessary for the bigger picture that you cannot currently see or understand. It doesn't matter if you're fifteen, twenty-five, thirty-five, or even forty-five-plus. It is never too late for God to restore and mend your heart. It is never too late for Him to bless you with the desires of your heart. You can move forward.

JOURNAL CHALLENGE

Check your heart! Are you holding on to past mistakes that hinder you from moving forward? God wants us to move forward and stop hanging on to our past hurts and mistakes. He wants to give you a future that is full of His love, kindness, mercy, grace, favor, and blessings, but you have to allow Him to come into your life. You have to accept Him and love Him with all your heart. So are you ready to give it all to God?

ACCEPT CHRIST INTO YOUR HEART

God, I accept You today in my heart as my Lord and Savior, Jesus Christ. I surrender myself to You. Fill me with Your Holy Spirit to help lead me in every area of my life. Thank You for sacrificing Your Son's life by dying on the cross so that You can save me from all my sins and mend my heart from brokenness. Thank You, Father, for first loving me. Thank You for Your mercy and grace. I choose You this day to dwell in me. In Jesus's name, amen.

REDEDICATE YOUR HEART TO CHRIST

God, forgive me of the sins I have committed. I choose this day to rededicate my heart to You. Thank You for loving me in my mess, rescuing me out of darkness, and giving me another chance to get it right. Thank You for allowing Your Son to die on the cross to save me from my sins, so that I might have everlasting life. I know I don't deserve it, and I do not take Your love for granted. Thank You for first loving me. I choose to give my heart to You from this day forward. In Jesus's name, amen.

AFTERWORD

This devotional has been a tremendous journey for myself. I pray that it has been a blessing to you, as it was for me. I encourage you to reflect on each section of this devotional. Think about each section challenge. Reflect on the journal entries you have written throughout this twelve-day journey, and really take in what God has said to you personally. I hope these challenges helped you pinpoint any areas in your life that have been broken in any way, and I pray that God mends your heart.

Printed in the United States
By Bookmasters